WE ARE HONORED TO HAVE THE ENDORSEMENTS FROM THE FOLLOWING PEOPLE...

"Susan never ceases to communicate in the most direct, yet gracious way! She has a real talent of telling it like it is and making us feel good about ourselves at the same time!"
Beccie Dawson
Chief People Officer, THINK Together

"Looking for a job? YOU need to read Susan Howington's book. Howington's years of experience in the field of Executive Outplacement, Coaching and Leadership Development translate into a guide on steps to avoid in sabotaging yourself. This simple yet brilliantly written primer will make a difference in your job search."
Beth Adkisson
Executive Coach & Chair, Vistage International, Inc.

"Susan's book is a quick and compelling read for any executive conducting a serious job search. She offers practical and common-sense wisdom distilled from many years of outplacement industry and networking experience. In today's fiercely competitive job market you need to maximize all the possible advantages to differentiate yourself from the competition. To ignore Susan's advice is to do so at your own peril and you will likely commit 'Mistake #12' in sabotaging your job search success!"
Bob Zierk
Senior Vice President, Global Human Resources, D&M Holdings

"My kudos to Susan Howington for telling it like it is! I found her shared wisdom to be insightful, straightforward and different than what is found in most books written on the subject of how to find a job. As a retained recruiter for over 30 years I wish more executives would take Susan's advice."

Brad Remilllard
Co-Founder, IMPACT Hiring Solutions
Co-Founder, American Association of Senior Executives (AASE)

"Susan has a very communicative and uplifting optimism, which is so appreciated and useful to people experiencing job search. Anybody in need of building or enhancing their own brand will find her strategies particularly effective."

Christian Bardin
VP International Sales and Marketing, Parfums de Coeur

"This book is a clear reflection of Howington's impeccable insight about the seemingly 'hidden' dynamics that occur in one's job search. These dynamics could in fact hinder or sabotage an executive's productivity, and ultimately, their ability to land the job they really want. I consider Susan an expert and a valuable resource to executives going through the job search journey."

David Holder
Founder, The Men in Transition (MIT) Group
Managing Director, Holder Capital Partners

"Emotions can override logic during a career transition. Susan Howington's years of experience offer real-life examples and practical sound advice, enabling her to provide readers with a common-sense approach for preparing, managing and landing their next career opportunity. This book is a must read for any executive, especially in today's competitive and challenging employment climate."

Howard Derman
Executive Vice President, Human Resources, Apria Healthcare Group

"Susan Howington offers expert advice, a high integrity approach to relationships, and genuine help from the heart for anyone who is trying to build a better personal brand. She could successfully offer this help in many business lines; executives in transition are darn lucky to have Susan's wisdom focused on their needs. Susan's words are a dose of reality and truth for leaders to understand how they can realize a more satisfying future of great relationships."

>*Jeff Black*
>*Partner, McDermott & Bull Executive Search*

"This extremely informative book gives practical, common-sense steps that readers need to do to show themselves in the best possible light during a job search. Your approach gives potential candidates a clear understanding of what to do, and not to do before, during and after an interview."

>*John Poracky*
>*President, AIMS Intl.-US-Midwest*
>*Executive Vice President, AIMS International Global Executive Search Firm*

"What they didn't teach you in B-school...but should."

>*Nancy L. Vanderlip*
>*HID Global Corporation*

"What a great read! This book is packed with insightful, practical advice that will help even the most accomplished high achiever turbo-charge their job search. Susan provides sound guidance based on her many years of experience helping executives successfully navigate the career transition process."

>*Steven A. L'Heureux*
>*CEO & President, Ryko Solutions, Inc.*

"Susan provides a substantive tool for any executive (or anyone for that matter) who wants straightforward advice. Susan's stellar background in outplacement and career coaching provide the platform for her to cut-to-the-chase wisdom. Her comments are insightful, honest, practical and right on!"

> *Terry Goldfarb-Lee,*
> *Senior Director of Business Development,*
> *Resources Global Professionals*

"Job search today is more challenging than ever before. What people need is practical and honest advice to help get them back to work as quickly as possible. This book provides the ground rules for ensuring that your job search creates positive and productive experiences for you and those that you encounter."

> *Veena Dua-Chillar*
> *Vice President, Global Human Resources, Specific Media*

"Job search is far from simple. Use this book to do a self assessment of your own behavior, attitude and communication style. You may be doing all the right things, but in the wrong ways!"

> *Wayne Wilkinson*
> *President & COO, McFarland Cascade*

"Susan Howington is a premier career coach with great insights into job search behavior. She has crafted a book that shows how individuals frequently behave in ways that are counterproductive to landing the job or the promotion they want."

> *William K Ellermeyer*
> *Principal, Ellermeyer Connect*

How Smart People SABOTAGE Their Job Search

10 Mistakes Executives Make and How to Fix Them!

Written by
Susan Howington

with
Diane Y. Chapman

Copyright © 2011 by Susan Howington
All rights reserved.

ISBN-10: 1466218347
EAN-13: 9781466218345

DEDICATED TO

My dad, Blair Chapman, who was a salesman of real estate,
cars and life insurance during his lifetime.
He enriched my life by instilling in me my interest
in human behavior and people-watching.
He gave me an appreciation for style and good taste.

My mom, Donna Lou Skjerven Chapman,
who gave me the best advice she could
about surviving in corporate business.
She was a high school English teacher, yet somehow,
she always had the right perspective.

My husband, Keith, who believed in my dream
and gave me the chance to pursue my business of
Power Connections and do what I love to do best.
This book and my business would not be in existence
today without his unwavering support.

My son, Christopher, who since he was a baby in a car seat,
has endured listening to thousands of my phone
conversations and has overheard me talk to hundreds
of executives about their job search.

ACKNOWLEDGEMENTS

I want to acknowledge some very special people, for these are people who demonstrated their support and encouragement to me as I ventured into entrepreneurialism and developed the Power Connections dream and business. I could not have come this far without their help:

Beth Adkisson has been my business coach and treasured advisor for over 10 years. As my Vistage Chair, she provided insightful guidance when I was running a business region for a global outplacement firm. Later, she gave me tools and the encouragement I needed to step out and launch Power Connections. She is an exceptionally talented business person and I am so grateful for her mentoring.

Diane Chapman is my Chief Writer and Communications Officer. She has been with me from the very beginning, acting as my cheerleader, confidant, and creative inspiration! She has willingly helped with anything I needed, taking on any role, big or small. I am so deeply grateful for her commitment to me and to the clients we have served through the years.

Dick Israel of Dick Israel Partners has been a business advisor and friend for many years. When I shared with him that I was on my own and that I had a service concept that was different than the other outplacement firms, without a second of hesitation he said, "Count me in!" He has been a tremendous support.

Jim Chapman has shown me continued support, always believing in my ability to create a business success story.

Mark Rhoades and I were members of Vistage together. While attending a Vistage holiday party, I don't remember exactly what I said, but it was some expression of insecurity about venturing out to start my own company. In response to my lamentation, Mark stated clearly and sincerely, "You worry too much!" Mark, you have no idea how those simple words have given me confidence during the past five years. Thank you, my friend!

Matt Sauer, an early Power Connections' customer, has also become a strategic advisor, giving me the corporate HR executive perspective when I need it.

Meredith Kaplan Burns for her editing expertise and for making the process of getting this book ready for publishing appear to be so easy!

Mike Wilson, of Viet Long Technologies, literally "gave me" a website and hours and hours of technical support when I didn't have the resources to establish an Internet presence. To this day, I am grateful for the support of Mike and his team.

Ruth Drizen-Dohs, of Drizen-Dohs Corporate Communications (DDCC), and her talented staff, in particular, Christina Jorgenson, have generously shared their talent, creative expertise, time and resources with me. Starting with sending a reporter from the *Los Angeles Times* to interview me after only being in business three weeks! Although I have had a lean marketing and public relations budget, I have always been treated like I was their biggest client. One day, I hope this is the reality!

Val Giannini is a Principal of NewCap Partners. The truth is, I have Val to thank for giving me the idea to create Power Connections.

Finally, I want to make a special acknowledgement of my dear business friend, Ken Bertok, who sadly passed away this year. Ken was an Executive Recruiter with the search firm of McCormick & Farrow. He was the consummate professional and one of our world's nicest people. Ken extended support to me and my clients from the beginning. I could always count on him to take my phone call, or meet me over breakfast to brainstorm about how to help a client in today's challenging job market.

HOW SMART PEOPLE SABOTAGE THEIR JOB SEARCH:

10 MISTAKES EXECUTIVES MAKE AND HOW TO FIX THEM!

TABLE OF CONTENTS

Introduction xv

Mistake # 1 1
We Forget the Importance of First Impressions.

Mistake # 2 21
We Make it Hard for Others to Feel Good About Helping Us.

Mistake # 3 35
We Communicate in Our "Executive Tone."

Mistake # 4 41
We Sabotage Our Job Search Before We are Even
Out of a Job by Being Rude to Outside Service Providers.

Mistake # 5 49
We Build a Network that Looks Just Like "Us."

Mistake # 6 55
We Don't Build a Network When We are Working.

Mistake # 7 59
We Change Our Elevator Speech.

Mistake # 8 65
We Expect Help to Come at No Cost to Us.

Mistake # 9 73
We Fail to Give Attention and Acknowledgment
To a "Less than Perfect" Reputation.

Mistake # 10 77
We Forget that the Interview Process Begins
in the Parking Lot.

Mistake #11 (A bonus tip for you!) 83
We Don't Believe that This Advice Will Work.

INTRODUCTION

If there is one thing we might all agree on it's that the overall measurement of success in a job search is whether or not we land a new job in the timeframe in which we expected. But I am of the opinion that the success of the job search process can also be measured by what we learn about ourselves. A measurement of success can also be determined by the relevant people we meet, and the meaningful relationships we create along the way. These new relationships can enhance our business and personal lives for years to come.

Job search can be one of life's greatest challenges. I know how hard people work at finding a new job; it is an ENORMOUS undertaking! It's grueling, it's tedious, and it's frustrating. By itself, it can be the most difficult "job" you've ever had! However you want to describe it, chances are I agree with your sentiments. Throughout this book, I would like to share observations I have made of executives going through this process. Perhaps I can shed some insight on what I have witnessed others doing that have potentially worked against them in their searches or at a minimum, held them back so that their searches took longer than they should have.

By sharing stories of my work with executives in transition through the years, you may gain some insight about yourself and what you are doing to support, or heaven forbid, sabotage your own job search. Either way, you will learn what to continue doing, and what to *stop* doing, and move forward with more confidence and more success.

Considering that the average tenure at any given company and for any given executive is 2.5–3.5 years, and that most of us won't stop working (commonly known as "retiring") until we are close to 70 years old, it is highly likely that an executive who is 55 years old today will work for another 10–15 years, and therefore, will work for another 3–4 more companies. If you are hearing this for the first time, it's a shocking revelation! It's why I wrote this book.

Inside I explain why the genesis of an effective job search actually starts while we are still employed! I have included examples of how our actions and behaviors while we are still employed can sabotage us when we are looking for new job opportunities.

I also describe why the ability to carry out an effective job search is critical to our professional future, our financial well-being, our life balance, and our general state of contentment. There are so many factors we face in our search over which we have no control. We've all experienced the good, the bad and the ugly about the job seeking process. Most of the time, we don't even know what is going on behind the scenes. We may not even know what we are up against, and even if we did, we may not be able to do anything about them.

So I say, in this very peculiar and uncomfortable stage of our professional lives, we take care to be in control of what we can,

INTRODUCTION

and pay attention to all of our actions, deemed big and small, during our searches, to ensure that we land a new job in the timeframe we expected. I hope this book will help you accomplish this critical goal.

MISTAKE #1

WE FORGET THE IMPORTANCE OF FIRST IMPRESSIONS.

"Life is too short to have anything but delusional notions about yourself."

Gene Simmons
Rock Star

I LAUGHED WHEN I READ THIS QUOTE! As much as I would like to believe in the humorous application of this statement, it only applies to rock stars, celebrities and others—not us! If we believe it's true, a delusional view of the professional impression we make on others can be the kiss of death (no pun intended here) to the success of our job search!

I think I am safe in making the assumption that if you are of executive status, you are accomplished in an area of expertise. You could probably say with all honesty, "I have been there, and done that in many areas of my particular focus and expertise."

So, you ask, "Should I worry about how I look and the way I'm dressed? I have proven myself time and again and I have the accomplishments clearly stated on my résumé. If someone doesn't like the way I look, too bad. Maybe they aren't worth my time, or maybe I don't want to work for that company."

Do you make the mistake of thinking you are not being judged by the way you look and how you are dressed? Think again. Some universal principles about job search must be acknowledged, or you risk sabotaging your search right out of the starting gate. Whether you are looking for a job, trying to build a consulting practice, trying to find investors for a business concept, or you are encouraging new customers to come through the doors of your new retail store, you need to dress nicely. When you are networking and promoting yourself or your ideas, the simple rule always applies: dress up versus down!

To be honest with you, I would really rather dress like a rock star! But if I did dress like a rock star, would you take me seriously? No! You would doubt my credibility and you would really wonder about me! I dress the way that I dress so I can be effective. I know my business. I am an expert in what I do, but if I came to my office dressed like a rock star, you probably wouldn't believe me…and I would not be able to help you like I know I can.

I once had a client who was a GM/divisional president level professional. He was a self-proclaimed maverick, meaning he tended to do his own thing and was a bit of a non-conformist. Which is okay…some cultures appreciate this type of characteristic. I arranged for him to network with a business friend of mine who is connected in spaces where I knew my client wanted to work. They made plans to meet for coffee.

My friend, who has a lot of class, didn't tell me that my client showed up for this coffee in jeans and a Hawaiian shirt. I figured this out afterwards by a few comments she made about their conversation. The fact was, this was a wasted contact for my client, because my friend was not going to open her proverbial rolodex for him—she couldn't afford to disrupt her reputation by taking a risk on my client with her treasured contacts. She operates in circles of the business community where people dress up rather than down. She wasn't going to give him an entree into this community knowing that he might arrive in a way that did not "show well."

It is essential that you look as credible and experienced as you say you are!

I had a client who I encouraged over and over again to either wear a suit and tie, or a dark sports coat, slacks and dress shirt, when he was networking. I suggested this because he was very much an introvert and he had a rather soft voice. He did not project a strong sense of self or leadership in his day-to-day demeanor. I believed that his clothing would help him create a stronger image.

I mentioned this to him on several occasions and even directly requested that he wear a particular dark suit and tie for an upcoming evening networking event. To my surprise, this client came to the event wearing a light-colored golf shirt and tan sports coat. Let me share the dynamics I witnessed in the room on that night: The executives who wore suits and ties all gravitated toward each other in one corner of the room. They all knew the executive status of each other by the way they were dressed.

My client, who was in the golf shirt and tan jacket, was an executive, but he did not gravitate over to this executive group. Now, my job is to make introductions at this venue, and even though I mentioned to this client my desire to introduce him to the executives in the "suited" group, it never happened that night. My client in the tan jacket was conveniently engaged in conversation with other "lower level" professionals during the networking hour, and I was not able to move him into the group of peers where he belonged.

I have a friend who works for a global financial services firm in downtown Los Angeles. When networking in a group, he looks for the men and women who are the *best dressed* in the room. Right or wrong, he believes that the "best dressed" implies the "most successful," and he wants to know successful people.

There is a gentleman with whom I am acquainted from conversations over the telephone when we discussed my services. He was looking for a GM or CEO spot with a small, privately held business in the technology industry.

We talked a few times and he concluded that he was doing fairly well building his network, making contacts and getting interviews. He decided that he would continue on his way without my assistance.

A few weeks later, I found myself sitting next to this same gentleman at a business meeting. My first "in person" impression of him was terrible. He simply looked sloppy. We subsequently saw each other a number of times at association meetings, and unfortunately, my image of him never changed. He is a technology industry slob.

I never had the opportunity to work with him but if I had, I would have provided him with what I thought would be invaluable feedback about his image.

If you want to be the boss, and be the leader, and be considered "executive status," you need to look like one. Most people are not so exceptionally brilliant, regardless of the industry they're in,

MISTAKE #1

to be "excused" from looking like a shlump. You must *always* remember this: You only get *one chance* to make a great first impression. Sorry, but this is a principle in life that has not changed over time.

As Keith Ferrazzi writes in his book, *Never Eat Alone*, "Image and identity have become increasingly important in our new economic order. With the digital sea swelling in sameness and overwhelmed in information, a powerful brand—built not on a product but on a personal message—has become a competitive advantage."

I find this statement to be particularly impactful. In a technical world where so much promotion of ourselves is done via the Internet versus in person, image and identity are critical success factors for us now, and into the future.

For the record: I know most of you think you know how to pull off a professional image. And, you probably do. But my point is, even though you know what you need to do, some of you *won't*! (I am writing this with a smile.) Right now, I know you are justifying your current look and wardrobe, and why these common image mistakes don't have relevance to you, your profession and your situation. Your heels are dug into the ground about this topic. Yes? If this is *you*, please stay with me and read on.

Professional Image 101

So what does a professional image look like? It isn't just charm, intelligence, charisma or Ivy League degrees that get us a job. Cherie Kerr, author of *How to BE Presidential: The Secret Handbook for Top-Level Executives and Those Who Aspire to Be*, states in her book, "Ask not what you can do for your image; ask what your image can do for you." Professional image—how we look, how we move, the intonation of our speech, our communication style—all present our professional image.

There is one caveat to these guidelines: I am always asked about how to dress for those companies that are extremely casual in their dress code. If you show up in a suit for an interview and everyone is in T-shirts, jeans and displaying their tattoos, I would say you didn't do your research very well. Just be smart about it. The idea is to fit in. It's not that hard! Do your research about the company like you normally would, and ask about the dress code for interviewing. Simple.

I believe your image is so important to your job search success that I am compelled to finish this chapter with a reminder of what we should all do to project our best executive selves. Bear with me as I continue…we'll get to the next chapters of this book soon enough.

But first, some critical reminders about:

Hair Cut and Color

The right cut and color of your hair can take years off of your appearance, and more importantly, give the impression that you are energetic, open to change, and "youthful" in your perspective.

Some career consultants are adamant that their "older" clients color their hair to hide the gray. If you decide to do this, your color needs to be done *well*, preferably by a professional stylist. Don't guess on this step! Do-it-yourself hair color that is bought at the grocery store works fine for some people, but looks really bad on many! Go to a hairstylist and review your options. Your hairstylist can be a terrific teammate for this process.

Hands

I'm so sorry to report this, but our hands are a dead giveaway to our age, our hygiene practices and our lifestyle. While you are at the salon getting your hair cut and colored, please think about getting regular manicures, too! Men, if you have not ever experienced a manicure, you will be surprised at how nice this feels. And by the way, people do notice when a man has nice hands and nails. Enough said.

Your Smile

The first smile you exchange with a prospective employer speaks volumes about you. Nothing says "I really take care of myself" more than healthy teeth and fresh breath. Right now, it's easier than ever to whiten and brighten our mouths and to troubleshoot halitosis!

If you haven't seen your dentist for six months or more, schedule a cleaning and a whitening consult. If you decide not to invest in dental office whitening, pick up a teeth-whitening kit from the drugstore, and start using it immediately. It's inexpensive, easy, and it will make a difference over time. If you have reoccurring bad breath, ask your dentist what you can do to alleviate the condition. I really want to stress the importance of taking impeccable care of your teeth, gums, and breath! Don't let your teeth or breath be the focus of someone's take-away impression of you—unless of course, they are left with an impression of your dazzling smile!

Eyeglasses

If you are still wearing eyeglass frames bought in the 1990s, or even early 2000s, make an appointment right away with an eyewear specialist to discuss a new look. Glasses make a statement about your interest in staying current, and being progressive. They can create an image for you of power, intellect, confidence and innovation. Whatever image you want to communicate, your glasses will help you do it.

Your Wardrobe

Ladies First...

We have it tough. Fashion changes constantly from year to year. Fortunately, if you make smart purchases to supplement your existing career wardrobe, many pieces can be worn as styles change and integrated into the new "current" looks. I admonish you, however, to err on the side of *style* versus the conservative or "outdated" side of your wardrobe.

In other words, make sure you have two suits that were purchased in the last two years. Do the same for pant and blazer coordinates. Make sure you have two current pairs of shoes that are office appropriate. Check your purse inventory. You'll need handbags that were purchased in the last two years, and are neutral in color. Jewelry should be simple and chic, and worn to complement an outfit and your hands. Too much jewelry, or jewelry that was once trendy but now is not, will distract from the contemporary image you are trying to project.

Now for Men...

You have it a little easier than women. However, if you haven't bought a new suit and a new sports coat in over five years, it's time to update your clothing investment. I am making an assumption that you regularly buy dress shirts, but if this is not the case, order some custom-made shirts, or replenish your shirt inventory with shirts of a good quality and proper fit.

Make sure you have two new suits, a navy or black blazer, slacks and a pair of current dress shoes in the closet. Belts need to be in nice condition and must match the color of your shoes. Invest in at least two new ties of excellent quality. These will add a touch of class and update your wardrobe. If you need assistance, most men's stores and men's departments in major retailers offer excellent wardrobe consulting advice.

Or better yet, hire an image consultant. You will be in great hands and will be on the mark with your wardrobe and image without question!

Note to both genders: If your weight has fluctuated since you purchased the clothes, please, *please* get your wardrobe tailored to fit your new size! Take the pants and coats in, or let the seams out, and do buy new dress shirts! It's not the time to delude yourself by thinking you'll lose weight to "fit back into" an older wardrobe before you land an interview. If you don't want to go through the trouble and expense of getting your clothes tailored, buy new replacements. ***Successful executives wear clothes that fit!***

Regarding Your Physical Condition

I won't go into great lengths to discuss this sensitive subject because this is a tough topic for most of us.

Now is the time to take charge of your health. Be honest with yourself, and "just do it." Your lifestyle habits are things that you do have control over in your job search, versus the many things in a job search that you can't control. You know who you are and what you need to do to appear healthy, energetic, and competitive in your marketplace. Just ask yourself, "Do I need to lose weight? Do I need to quit smoking? Do I need to adopt a healthier diet? Am I exercising enough?" If you need help with any of these, hire a personal trainer, a smoking cessation expert, or a nutritionist. Your doctor can help you find the right professional support.

In Jeffrey Meshel's book, **One Phone Call Away: Secrets of a Master Networker**, he has a chapter entitled *Perception of Self, How Others See Us*. In this chapter he states, "The perception may be wrong, but it doesn't matter. Perception is reality." He goes on to write, "This just means you should be mindful of presenting yourself in the best possible way you can. You cannot skimp when it comes to your attire, and, of course, you should choose your accessories wisely. Buy clothes that make you look as presentable as possible. Because the first thing someone sees is your physical appearance. They have an immediate reaction. They draw an instant conclusion, fair or unfair, right or wrong. That's reality. And if you can put yourself in the most advantageous position with that first perception, it's going to pay dividends."

First Impressions Also Apply to How We Come Across Via Telephone and Email

With all the phone interviews that are going on these days, this is really, really important!

If you are a person with low energy, or have been known to have a depressive personality, or if you're a person who tends to wear their emotions on their sleeve, chances are, your phone presence may indicate this. I am not trying to be harsh here. You know who you are, and I want to help you so you can modify your communication style so it works in your favor, and not against you.

I had lunch not too long ago with a friend of mine who is President of her own insurance brokerage firm. As President, she is

MISTAKE #1

still intimately involved with the hiring process, as it is vitally important to her business to hire people with the right skills and fit.

She was sharing a story with me about making a call to a candidate they were considering for hire. However, because she didn't like the way he answered the phone, she immediately hung up on him! I laughed at the thought of this actually happening, and asked her if she really did, in fact, hang up on the guy. She replied, "Absolutely!" Her point was that if they are this way even once, she can't afford to have someone with a bad attitude or low energy give a less-than-stellar image of her company on the phone to customers, or anyone else for that matter.

So, what are we talking about here? Let me give you a couple of examples. By the way, the names in these examples are fictitious.

> *Ring, Ring...*
> Joanne: "Hello?"
> Caller: "Hi, is this Joanne?"
> Joanne: "Yes."
> Caller: "Hi Joanne, this is John from ABC Recruiting Firm. I am calling you about a search I'm doing for a VP of Finance."
> Joanne: "Oh. Hi."

This level of energy makes me wonder if Joanne is motivated to work, and if she is really *not* happy to hear from the recruiter. It makes me wonder all kinds of things about Joanne's personality and situation. If I were Joanne, and looking for a job, I would be happy to hear from *any* recruiter, and I would demonstrate it in my voice and the energy level of my conversation. Taking this a step further, *I would answer every call as if I was expecting it to be a potential employer or recruiter on the other end.*

I will never forget the time that I returned the phone call of a gentleman who was interested in learning more about how my company could help him with his job search. The call went like this:

> *Ring, Ring…*
> Mike answers: "WHAT!" (He yells.)
> Me: "Mike, (I hesitate) it's Susan Howington."
> Mike: "WHO?" (He yells.)
> Me: "Susan Howington. I'm returning your call. Have I caught you at a bad time?" (No kidding!)
> Mike: "Oh!…Oh!…Susan! I am so sorry; I thought you were my wife calling me. We had a fight this morning, and I'm still reeling from it. Yes, I had some questions I wanted to ask you…"

Now, I had several thoughts about this guy when he and I began to talk:

- First, assuming he can see the caller's phone number on his cell phone, one would think he would know if his wife is calling him or not.

- Second, if I was a hiring corporate executive, or a recruiter calling to talk to him, I would not pursue this guy as a candidate. Period. Too risky.

MISTAKE #1

- Third, if I were a networking contact calling to set up a coffee meeting to discuss leads and target companies, I would think twice about using this person as a reference resource to support my candidacy in target companies where he may have contacts. Who really knows what his professional reputation is in his business circle?

- Fourth, I thought about how my friend who owns the insurance brokerage firm would have hung up on him.

If he was my client, I would have given him the feedback that when his cell phone rings, he needs to be sure to look at the number of the calling party. If the phone number isn't recognizable, then assume it is a hiring company or recruiter calling you, and "turn on the great first impression!" Make sure your voice projects a happy, balanced, competent person.

So, be cognizant of your phone persona! Think about the image you have created in the minds of those who hear you, but cannot see you. Answer your cell phone as if you were at work. Most of us answer our calls with a professional greeting, like "Good morning, this is Susan." Don't let down your professional persona, not even for one phone call. Consider each call as a step taking you closer to employment.

Voicemail

Make sure your voicemail depicts your professional self as well. For example, "Hi, this is George James. I'm sorry I missed your call. Please leave a message and I will get back to you shortly." It's short, to the point, but pleasant. And, oh yes, a word of advice: leave your creative side out of this. I encourage you to change your voicemail if you are coming across as too casual.

For example, no "Hey's," "Yo's," or benign messages like "It's me, leave a message." No long music interludes making someone wait before they can leave a message. This can be a time waster, and the music selection and quality may not appeal to the caller. No singing your voicemail message in opera or any other style, unless you are really a great singer, then maybe.... Don't try to be clever. Your teenage son and his friends come up with the clever voicemail messages—not you.

Message Machines

Most people use their cell phone as their primary phone number when in job search. But if you list your home phone number, I advise you to consider the following guidelines:

As much as I adore the sweet voices of small children, and as much as I am crazy about animals, if your message has one or both reciting a greeting, please, *please* make sure it is easily understood, and that it is actually really cute, not silly. If in doubt, just change your message to a simple, "This is the Smith family, sorry we can't come to the phone right now. Please leave a message and we'll call you back."

After your job search is over, you can put your recording of Sparky barking to the tune of jingle bells back on your machine.

If you list your home phone number on your job search documentation, it is very important that whoever answers your phone represents you well and can take an accurate message. This is the time to train your kids on good telephone etiquette. If you have relatives in your home who are not known for taking good messages, then it's best to create a policy to let the phone ring and have the answering machine pick it up. If 15-year-old Emily is totally bored with everyone else's business but her own, and has a tendency to reflect this in her phone personality, then tell Emily not to answer the family phone when you aren't there.

Have you ever called a business to ask for directions and the person who answered the phone didn't speak English? Did you wonder why the proprietor would let someone answer the phone who couldn't represent the business well? Simply stated, your job search is a business affair. It is best that relatives from the Old Country who don't speak fluent English, or Grandpa, who is slightly deaf, or five-year-old Jimmy, not interact with your potential employer, recruiters or others who are contacting you about your job search.

Finally, A Note About Email…

Your email address should also be professional. Surfingirl@yahoo.com, emilysgrandma@cox.net, budsboy@gmail.com, screamingdemon@rr.socal.com and other expressive email addresses like these should be changed for your job search. Remember, these addresses will be put at the top of your résumé, on your business card, and on other marketing documents in your job search. You don't want someone making a judgment about your abilities based on your alter-ego email address. Alleviate this risk from the beginning. It is not hard to establish a new email address for your search, and you want your email address to reflect your best professional self during this time. Just use your name, or a derivative of your first and last name, for your new email address. You can always use your original one for your personal email communication.

Or perhaps you believe that email is the new method of sending "thank you's" to prospective employers? Rethink that strategy. Never underestimate the power of a hand-written note.

Oops! How to Fix Mistake #1:

Honestly? Mistake #1 has so many ways to sabotage your job search; it's like walking through a mine field. "You never get a second chance to make a great first impression." However, you can certainly try. If your gut is telling you that you hit a land mine in your phone call, or miscalculated your style of interview clothing, regroup and consider re-communicating your interest in a job or networking opportunity. Having the backbone to correct and reach out again speaks volumes to potential companies. Seek professional help from a career management coach or wardrobe consultant. Course corrections are in order any time, and it's better to make the corrections early in your job search process rather than later.

Mistake #1 Self-Assessment and Improvement Plan

Stand in front of the mirror. Seriously. Stand there and take a good, hard look from head to toe. Then answer these questions based upon what you see:

1. Are there any aspects of your personal physical image that you need to work on? Here, I'll help you. Check all that apply:
   _____Hair cut and color?
   _____Hands?
   _____Teeth?
   _____Eyeglass frames?
   _____Weight?
   _____And for the ladies—makeup application?

2. Have you updated your wardrobe recently to make sure you are "interview-ready?"

MISTAKE #1

Ladies first!
_____Suits?
_____Shoes?
_____Handbag?
_____Jewelry?
_____How about the fit? Is everything tailored appropriately?

Gentlemen? How about you?
_____Suits?
_____Shoes?
_____Belts?
_____Ties?
_____Fitted shirts?
_____Everything tailored appropriately?

3. Do you need to update your appearance with a hair stylist, dentist, wardrobe consultant, tailor or personal trainer? Ladies, do you need to update your makeup use?

_____
_____
_____
_____
_____
_____

4. Ask a friend or coach to listen to your telephone persona, your voicemail and your home message machine. What image does your telephone demeanor portray? Do you come across in a professional and energetic way in your voicemail message? Does your

message machine greeting support this image as well? Do you need to make changes?

_____
_____
_____
_____
_____
_____

5. Have you established a "professional" personal email address yet?

_____
_____
_____
_____
_____
_____

6. One more thing: Have you purchased some professional "thank you" note cards yet? Handwritten notes can differentiate you from the other candidates. It takes more time to do, but it creates a lasting impression with the interviewer.

_____
_____
_____
_____
_____
_____

Based upon your assessment, utilize the tips within this chapter to improve and polish your "First Impression."

Additional Notes:

MISTAKE #2

WE MAKE IT HARD FOR OTHERS TO FEEL GOOD ABOUT HELPING US.

"When you are asking for what you want, take into account what the other person can give. Overplay your hand and you're likely to come up empty handed."

Harvey Mackay

I WILL TELL YOU HOW THIS HAPPENS. In Mistake #1, we talked about the importance of making a great first impression, and how we can ask for assistance from professionals to help us. Now, you need a few words about making sure your requests for help are received affirmatively. The bottom line on this mistake is that sometimes "you must get out of your own way."

We come across as being too picky.

I had become reacquainted with a former co-worker who was in need of a job. He told me about his financial situation and some other unfortunate personal circumstances that were pretty heartbreaking. I felt sorry for him and decided to keep my eyes open for relevant job leads for him as I went about my business.

Soon after our initial meeting, I was delighted to discover a job lead that I thought was perfect for him! I got excited about this lead because I also knew people who worked for the hiring company. I believed that I could arrange for him to get an endorsement by one of my friends associated with the company.

The job description stated that only local candidates would be considered. When he read this, he decided that he would be eliminated because he lived 50 miles from the company, and the long commute would be a strike against him. I pointed out to him, however, that he would be driving against the rush hour traffic patterns, thereby reducing commute time.

My interpretation of this statement about only "locals" was entirely different. I believed it to mean that they would not consider anyone out of state or an interested candidate that would have to relocate on their own initiative. I encouraged him to apply anyway, because after all, he could take the commuter train if he didn't want to drive. We had two totally different interpretations of the selection criteria. He was convinced, however, that *his* interpretation was right and therefore, he did not even apply. *I* interpreted his interpretation as "he didn't want to work so far away from home."

Two weeks later, I sent another job lead to this gentleman. Overall, he was a good fit for the job. The job description listed 20 criteria of desired requisites. Quite frankly there were a couple of requirements listed that I didn't fully understand, but I sent the lead to him anyway.

His response back to me was that since he didn't have the experience listed in criterion # 19, there was no point in pursuing the lead.

I think you know what I am going to write now. I never sent this gentleman another lead. As badly as he needed to work, he found reasons not to even apply for the job leads sent to him. Go figure.

This is a good segue into the next point.

We express criticism of job leads that are sent to us versus expressing appreciation.

This is a slam-dunk. How should we handle a job lead that is sent to us by someone in our network, yet is *way out in left field*, or a smidgeon off-base? How about sending back the reply: "It was very considerate of you to think of me. Thank you very much for this lead—I will let you know if anything transpires."

No need to go into detail or explanation about the lead. Just show appreciation for their kind gesture. After all, people don't need to extend their time and attention to us, so let them know that *you* know they are going out of their way to help you.

We "over-communicate" what it is that we are looking for and we overload people with directions on how they can help us.

When this happens, you have just wasted your breath, and their time. They have stopped listening, or they are in overload, and now they don't know what it is you want. They will second-guess and question if they will be able to provide any meaningful assistance to you at all.

In 15-plus years of being in the career transition industry, I have politely endured many a monologue about what someone wants, what they *don't* want, how much they think they should earn versus what they have been getting, what kind of leadership they seek, what kind of culture they excel in, what kind of culture they *don't* excel in, how far they will or won't travel, their definition of upward mobility, and more. "Blah, blah, blah, *blah*."

My personal take away from this type of meeting is minimal… *very* minimal. If we become too prolific in our description of wants and needs we will lose our listening audience.

So the bottom-line with this point is: Have a great, concise elevator speech! Then expand on this, if asked, and keep it crisp for your listening audience. Show sincere enthusiasm and appreciation for the job leads and ideas that they pass your way. People will bend over backward for you if you show your appreciation.

We assume that people are thinking about us—and they aren't!

Don't feel bad. They aren't thinking about me either. This section is a "reality check." It's a reminder to you that all of your contacts and potential networking resources are extremely busy trying to juggle their own professional responsibilities and goals.

So how do we remind them to think about us? No, not by sending an email that says, "Just checking in…have you heard of any marketing job leads for me?" "Have you thought of any other contacts that would be good for me to meet?" Or "Do you know of any other companies that would fit my target profile?"

MISTAKE #2

Here is an email I received from an executive I had never met, or at least I cannot recall ever meeting him. Obviously, he didn't make any impression at all, let alone a good one with me, if we *had* met. He was requesting that I keep my eyes open for job opportunities for him. I have edited the email to make it more succinct, but the general message was kept the same as it was intended by the sender.

Dear Susan,

It has been awhile so I thought I'd reconnect with you as you suggested. I know it is hard to believe, but I am still waiting for a great opportunity and therefore I continue to be available to explore leads you may send my way.

As I told you before, I am looking for high-profile global companies to work with as a CEO or President. I am relocate-able to "real" metropolitan cities such as Los Angeles, Dallas, Chicago, New York, but not to places like Fargo, North Dakota; Little Rock, Arkansas; Cincinnati, Ohio; or any third-world countries for that matter. Truth be told, I have had a few opportunities that I've turned down because I didn't like the location.

Just wanted to make sure I was still on your radar. I've attached both a résumé and a bio, which are not current, but I didn't want to waste any time getting them out to my network.

Thanks,

Blatant Egocentric

I find this egregious message to be particularly presumptuous for numerous reasons:

1. I don't know the guy, so it isn't possible that I requested that he circle back with me.

2. Obviously this is a form letter, but if it weren't it would serve him well to remind me where we met to provide some association.

3. The "I know it is hard to believe" statement about still being out of work is pompous, to say the least.

4. He makes sure we know he wants a "high-profile global job." More pompousness!

5. He doesn't tell me what industries or what kind of specific businesses he is targeting, so how can I really help him?

6. Am I supposed to remember all the cities where he wants to work?

7. Well, *excuse me*, but Little Rock or Fargo may be my hometown. (And then to mention third-world countries in the same sentence makes me really wonder if I should be insulted.)

8. He wants to make sure he is still on my radar? He was never on my radar!

9. Why would he send me an out-of-date résumé? If you are going to go to the trouble of enlisting people's help, for Pete's sakes, represent your best self in the documentation that you are circulating.

Conversely, here is an email message from an executive I *do* know and who is sending his monthly message out to his network to keep them informed of his job search progress.

> Dear friends,
>
> Once again time has passed quickly since my last update. Thank you for the introductions, leads and sound advice. I am currently somewhere in the hunt on four different opportunities. The way employers are behaving today, it is difficult to say whether we are close or not. As you know, they are being quite selective about requirements. Of course, moving into the holiday season, things will slow down. But we march on.
>
> As you may know, I am a part-time instructor at a local junior college. It's been very rewarding and keeps me current in the financial and business literature. I do continue to look for permanent positions such as CFO, VP Finance and CAO. However, if you know of anyone who has experience teaching finance, accounting or similar courses, and would like to teach at the junior college level, please pass my name along and I will try to help them out.
>
> No need to respond, I just wanted to stay on your radar.
>
> Merry Christmas to you and your family,
>
> Conscientious

Keeping with the "staying on my radar" theme, it is not hard to read the difference in the tone of this message over the first message from Blatant Egocentric. Here is how one recruiter responded to the message from Conscientious.

From: A Recruiter
To: Conscientious
Re: Senior Financial Executive - Update

You know, Conscientious, I have been recruiting in this town for financial professionals for over 15 years. You are a smart and rare candidate. You understand how to stay in touch with recruiters, and do it in a professional, *while showing value,* kind of way. You would be shocked at how most people just don't understand that.

Thank you for the constant contact, and please continue to do so, as I will certainly call you first when I get anything close to your background.

Sincerely,

A Recruiter

Could you ask for a better response from a recruiter? My friend accomplished what he set out to do. He connected with someone of influence and won this person over to his side. I have no doubt that this recruiter will consider him the next time he has a CFO search.

And now, to determine your level of sensitivity and awareness of the capacity of others to help you, I present you with a short Networking Awareness Pop Quiz:

Networking Awareness Pop Quiz

Answer the following question:

A message with a "this is all about me" tone and a direct request for help may go unanswered because:

A. The recipient is too busy to answer.
B. The recipient is doing last-minute follow up for us before they respond.
C. They are embarrassed that they haven't done anything else to help us.
D. They are put off by our presumptuousness that we think we are the only thing they have to think about!

Answer: Is probably "D"

Did you get it right? Congratulations, you have an appropriate level of awareness of your contacts' capacity to help you.

We act overly presumptuous.

A business leader in Orange County recommended that a friend of hers, who was returning to work after having kids, give me a call to network.

Out of respect for the business leader, I was happy to oblige and eager to assist. The fact was, the woman who was reaching out to me was not only being too picky about what would constitute a job worthy of her talents, she also wanted to work for a company that would accept her re-entry into the corporate world after a five-year hiatus, and allow her flexibility to tend to her children while paying her a six-figure salary. I thought she was asking for more than a hiring company could give, nevertheless, I spent a great deal of time with her on the phone, brainstorming about industries and specific businesses she could approach.

Two weeks later, she called me out of the blue while I was preparing for a meeting with a major customer. She began the call with, "You said you would try to think of companies where my skills and work life/balance desires would fit in. Are there any other companies that you have thought of that I should approach since you and I last talked?" I was completely unprepared for the conversation, and was taken aback at how presumptuous she was! So much so, I felt resentment that she had put me on the spot. I had to be direct with her and said, "I am sorry but I don't have any other companies to suggest for you." Not only did I feel she was expecting too much from me, but I sensed that she was taking advantage of the referral. Hello!

By communicating in this direct, "this is all about me" manner, we turn people off, and we put them in an embarrassing position. We put them in the position where they have to admit, "No, I haven't given any more thought to you and your search." By being too presumptuous about our expectations of others' offers to help, and their time, we can actually embarrass the very person from whom we are seeking help. We put them in an uncomfortable position.

Oops! How to Fix Mistake #2:

Communicate with graciousness—always, and without fail, in written and verbal communications and under all circumstances.

Before you hit the "send" button on your emails, ask a trusted friend or family member to review the messages, and ask for their honest opinions of the emails' tone and requests. When you are making follow-up calls to connections, use a polite greeting and ask if the timing of your call will fit into their schedule. Then, graciously allow them to respond about their availability.

Mistake #2 Self-Assessment and Improvement Plan

As with Mistake #1, there are oh so many ways we can be challenged with Mistake #2. Let's cover just a few of them:

1. Are you a picky person who is quick to dismiss leads and potential job interviews because they don't appear to "match" what and where you have in mind for your next position?

_____
_____
_____
_____
_____

2. Have you ever expressed criticism of a job lead, given to you by a helpful contact?

3. Do you tend to overload people with long monologues about what you are looking for?

4. Are you presumptuous and assuming when you approach people, believing that they are thinking about you, when in actuality, they are not?

Additional Notes:

MISTAKE #3

WE COMMUNICATE IN OUR "EXECUTIVE TONE."

"The less you speak of your greatness, the more I shall think of it."

Henry Ford

IT IS NOT UNCOMMON FOR ME TO see an executive who is highly assertive as one of their behavioral traits. It is also not uncommon to see that in addition to being assertive, some executives rate fairly *low* in their propensity to be helpful to others. This is not surprising to me, because let's face it, in order to rise to the executive ranks, they must assert themselves—and *continue* to assert themselves in order to stay at the top. Since executives are usually catered to, they become less apt to be accommodating and helpful to others. It only follows that they excel in "giving orders." They grow accustomed to being helped, versus being help*ful.*

If we relate this to an executive in job search mode, however, those that are high in assertiveness and low in helpfulness have a more difficult time in networking and job search activities. However, an executive who is high in "assertiveness," and high s;" or low in assertiveness, and high in helpful- is more successful at networking overall, be- 'rstand how to *give* and come across as helpful

Another trait or behavior where we can run into trouble is our communication style. A key factor in how effective an executive is in their communication skills is their propensity to be blunt, upfront and forthright, versus their propensity to be diplomatic. Ideally, if you are high in bluntness, you also want to be high in diplomacy.

So, let's say we have someone who is high in assertiveness, low in helpfulness, high in the blunt communications category, and low in their tendency to be diplomatic. Can this combination of traits predict how adept they'll be at the networking process? Can this combination of traits affect how happy or satisfied they'll be with the outcome of their networking efforts? How successful can a person be with networking if these are their traits? It's worth considering.

Do you agree with the following assumptions?

- As executives and people of management, we are used to *speaking*, and in return, having people listen to us.

- We are also used to people doing what we ask, or anticipate what we may need.

- We are accustomed to communicating in a way that exudes authority or some form of commandment.

- Since we are high in being assertive and low in being helpful, we are *not* used to doing things for others; we are used to others doing things for us.

MISTAKE #3

- Since we value forthright conversation, in other words, being to the point and blunt, we use this same communication style in our daily lives and with our network.

- And, finally, we are used to people responding to our every call.

Considering these behaviors, how are we doing? Countless executives have told me they are not ready to begin their job search and the prerequisite networking because they don't want to be accountable to give back.

If we use this same direct, commanding tone with our contacts and network, we could potentially destroy or minimize the outflow of resources that this network could, and hopefully should, provide us.

There is a gentleman who networks with me via email on a fairly regular basis. He understands that in order to get help, he needs to *give* help so every now and then, he sends me a job lead that I can pass on to my clients, or to send to someone else. But by nature, he is really a "command and control" type of communicator. I can tell that he just struggles when it comes to being patient during this whole career transition process.

He recently sent a job lead to me and I graciously replied back, saying that one of my clients may be a good fit. In response to my thank you message, he simply wrote back, "I need to be networking with that client." His communication style is very much to the point, obviously. You know, my reaction to that short and curt message was, "Yes, you and he should probably be networked with each other, and I will introduce you when I am good and ready." In other words, "Don't boss me around. I am not accountable to you." I admit, his communication style may not be intended to come across as abrupt, but as the recipient of the message, I have no way of knowing if he is being bossy or just clueless about how he comes across.

If he had said in his email something like, "Is there any possibility that you could introduce me to Joe?" or better yet, "Glad that this job lead can be of use. Sounds like a guy I would like to know. Would you mind making an introduction?" my reaction would have been, "You got it! Consider it done...Joe meet John; John meet Joe."

So, executives in transition, I want to caution you about the tone and the words that you use when asking others for their help. It may very well not be your nature to communicate with helpfulness or diplomacy. If you feel this is hindering your networking effectiveness, consider seeking advice from a career coach or leadership development coach.

Oops! How to Fix Mistake #3:

If you are not working, you are not the boss of the generous people with whom you network, or of whom you make requests. Your network is not accountable to you. They are not thinking about you. They don't have the time to work on your behalf. They will resent you if your communication style reflects an expectation of anything contrary to this fact. This may be difficult for you, but learn to communicate with helpfulness and accommodation.

Quite honestly, the answer to successful networking may be very simple. How do you get others to help you, and get them to think about you? Use honey to attract the bees. Sweeten up your communication style. Offer help to them...go beyond the statement, "If I can help you in any way, just let me know." Actually *think* of ways to help others.

Add your "please" and "thank you's." Add any other gracious and polite language that acknowledges that "they don't have to do anything" for you and you know it!

Your future depends on it!

Mistake #3 Self-Assessment and Improvement Plan

1. Have you looked closely at your own traits that can sabotage your job search? What are they?

   _____
   _____
   _____
   _____
   _____

2. Are you high in assertiveness, and low in helpfulness? How can you add balance to your traits?

   _____
   _____
   _____
   _____
   _____

3. Is your communication style considered blunt and commanding? How has that affected your job search?

   _____
   _____
   _____
   _____
   _____

Additional Notes:

MISTAKE #4

WE SABOTAGE OUR JOB SEARCH BEFORE WE ARE EVEN OUT OF A JOB BY BEING RUDE TO OUTSIDE SERVICE PROVIDERS.

"The best way to appreciate your job is to imagine yourself without one."

Oscar Wilde

Or, to be absolutely direct about this:

"To remind yourself to be respectful to vendors when you are employed, just imagine yourself unemployed."

Susan Howington

WHEN I ACT AS AN AGENT for my clients, I call executive recruiters to see if they would be kind enough to meet with a client of mine when I think it would be beneficial for them. Sometimes a recruiter will refuse the invitation. They refuse because they remember that five years ago, the executive "snubbed them," blew them off, asked for their help and then went and gave a paid search to the competition, asked for their advice and then never had the courtesy to return a phone call, or to thank them, or…the list goes on.

I am not talking about not returning phone calls from vendors or service providers; I am talking about being rude or disrespectful. As a service provider, I am trained to go after the business even if the business is from someone or a company that I don't personally find favorable. But to be truthful, we are all just human beings. Our feelings get hurt, we can become offended, and we can feel disrespected just like anyone else.

When you are in search you really need the help of the vendor and service provider community to source job leads for you…you REALLY do! And the great news is they have a vested interest in helping you! If they identify a position in a company, and help you get in the door, it is pretty likely that you will pay them back somehow by giving them business or by referring business to them.

You should be aware of another dynamic that is going on behind the scenes: Vendors and service providers talk to each other. We know which customers are difficult, who takes advantage of business arrangements, and who is nice to us when they need something, and rude to us when they don't. This is reality.

We also know those customers who, when they are in transition, are full of hugs and kisses, and when they land, they don't want anything to do with us.

Considering that vendors and service providers are only human after all, we can only go through this unhealthy dynamic a couple of times before we wise up and decide "we aren't going

MISTAKE #4

to take it" anymore. Therefore, any previous effort to help that person with their job search will very likely be discontinued.

Some people really don't see their behavior towards the vendor community as being egregious. To help you make a determination of your reputation within this segment of the business community, please review the following checklist:

Do any of the following describe you?

_____It is not uncommon for you to ask that a product or service be provided to you for free to give the vendor an opportunity entrée into your company. (The proverbial promise to help them get their foot in the door.)

_____You pride yourself in your negotiating techniques because you start the negotiations with ridiculously low pricing requests.

_____You are a Score Keeper. Do you insinuate to your vendor community that your relationship with them is conditional? Meaning, "I bought from you so now I expect you to do something for me," or "I did you a favor and threw a piece of business your way, so now you owe me…"

_____Do you accept nice gifts from vendors and neglect to say "Thank you" either by way of email, handwritten note or phone call?

_____Are you frequently rude to vendors who are trying to sell you something?

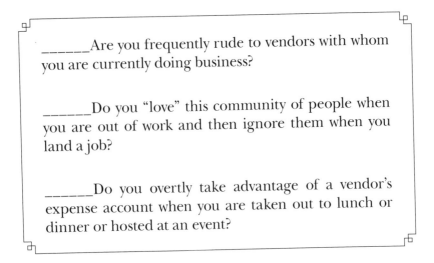

_____Are you frequently rude to vendors with whom you are currently doing business?

_____Do you "love" this community of people when you are out of work and then ignore them when you land a job?

_____Do you overtly take advantage of a vendor's expense account when you are taken out to lunch or dinner or hosted at an event?

If you answered "YES" to any of the above, there is a good chance that you need to mend a relationship fence. If you answered "YES" to several items above, it is highly probable that your reputation is damaged and you are being talked about negatively in the vendor community.

You may have all kinds of reasons to justify why you behave the way you do toward vendors, suppliers and professional service providers. But your justification is irrelevant. No one enjoys being misused, disrespected, talked down to, taken advantage of, unappreciated and treated poorly. Vendors are people and people are not perfect. But, I guarantee you, that at least 95% of the time, this kind of behavior was never justified to begin with.

Oops! How to Fix Mistake #4:

Always be open to meeting new people when you are working and be sure to know your vendors and service providers. Cultivate positive relationships with this community of businesspeople. Go to lunch with them, take their phone calls, and give them referrals for new business. At the very minimum, be kind and courteous. This you can do, and it will keep you off the "bad customer/client/prospect" list in the vendor and service provider community.

Mistake #4 Self-Assessment and Improvement Plan

1. Do you need to express more appreciation for the help others have given you? Are there people you need to circle back with and thank them for their acts of support? Write down the names of individuals with whom you'd like to reconnect to show appreciation.

   _____
   _____
   _____
   _____
   _____

2. Write down what you can do going forward to show or express your appreciation.

   _____
   _____
   _____
   _____
   _____

3. Are there fences you need to mend in the service provider community? How can you mend them?

   _____
   _____
   _____
   _____
   _____

4. Identify the vendor or service provider relationships that need your special attention.

   _____
   _____
   _____
   _____
   _____

Additional Notes:

MISTAKE #5

WE BUILD A NETWORK THAT LOOKS JUST LIKE "US."

"Don't join an easy crowd. You won't grow. Go where the expectations and the demands to perform are high."

> Jim Rohn
> *The Treasury of Quotes*

I LOVE THE SIMPLICITY OF THIS QUOTE. Job search is complicated, this I do know. And yet, I also know that we can involve ourselves in too many activities that take us away from the basics of an effective job search.

I always challenge my clients to spend equal time in a variety of networking situations. For every transition group they attend, I would like them to have a meeting with a working contact, or attend a business meeting that is not known as a transition group for the unemployed.

I was once told by a gentleman who was out of work that it was pointless to network with working people, because, he stated, they aren't looking for work and therefore have no job leads to share. I am still stunned by this rationale! Working people, after all, are getting called by recruiters. Just as diversity in the workforce is important to the growth and maturity and evolution of a business, the diversity of our network is also important.

Never pass up the opportunity to meet new people! However, keep in mind that networking is not just a collection of a massive amount of names and contact information. Networking should be done with purpose and a well-defined agenda. The idea is not to see how many people you can put into your database, or add to your LinkedIn connections, but to compile a list of people who will be happy to help you. I agree with Harvey Mackay when he says, "Networking is not a numbers game. The idea is not to see how many people you can meet; the idea is to compile a list of people you can count on."

Likewise, diversify the *types* of transition groups you attend. If you're a marketing manager who is attending nothing but groups for out-of-work marketing professionals, your strategy basically locks you into a network of your own competition. Misery definitely does love company, but it won't land you a job.

Build your network as part of your strategy to find work. Use networking as a thread that joins the fabric of your strategy. Too many people get caught up in what I call the "ether" of networking. They are so delighted in the friendliness of those in transition, and the attention they get from others in transition, that they begin to lose focus; they settle for *networking as their entire job search strategy* instead of using it as one of the bricks that builds the step to finding a job.

Oops! How to Fix Mistake #5:

Have an appreciation for people who fill different functions and who work in different industries than you. These people often know people who will be important to your job search later.

Seek out opportunities to network with professionals from diverse occupations. Even though we may fill a specialized job function and title, and have a definitive industry in which we've built our reputation, none of us works in a vacuum. Diversity in our networking can pay great dividends toward our future success.

Next time you find yourself questioning whether or not to meet a new group of executives at an event, remember: Diversity in your networking brings diversity to the list of people you may be able to count on.

Mistake #5 Self-Assessment and Improvement Plan

Take this opportunity to write down the ways you can diversify your network.

1. First, write down the professional associations or business meetings you have never attended, and research their meeting dates:

   _____
   _____
   _____
   _____
   _____

2. Next, identify people you need to meet outside of the transition community, or outside of your functional area, who could be valuable contacts in your job search plan:

   _____
   _____
   _____
   _____

3. Finally, set a goal to add these new activities and meetings to your weekly calendar. Record here dates and times you can set to reach out to these people, organizations and businesses.

   _____
   _____
   _____
   _____

4. BONUS POINTS: Better yet, set the goal that I challenge my clients with, and meet a working person, or attend a business association or business meeting, for every transition or networking function on your calendar. You will be amazed at how your network will evolve! How can you kick off this goal?

   _____
   _____
   _____
   _____

Additional Notes:

MISTAKE #6

WE DON'T BUILD A NETWORK WHEN WE ARE WORKING.

"No one—not rock stars, not professional athletes, not software billionaires, and not even geniuses—ever make it alone."

Malcolm Gladwell

THIS WILL SPEAK TO MANY OF YOU: Did you interact with outside vendors while filling the role in the corner office? Did you delegate the management of corporate relationships, vendors and customer relationships to your direct reports? Considering that vendors, professional service providers, and former customers can be our greatest source of job leads when we are looking, this is a huge mistake. Does this statement trigger an *"Oops"* for you?

None of us works in a vacuum. If you don't personally know members of the outside counsel that your firm uses, the presidents of your biggest customers, bankers that your CFO is interacting with, and other important outside resources, you are missing out. These people are connected! Their success depends on their connectivity in the business community at large. If they don't have a personal relationship with you, let alone actual experience *working* with you, you won't get the fullest benefit of their potential resources when you might need them the most.

Oops! How to Fix Mistake #6:

Get out and circulate in the business community at large. Don't isolate yourself within the walls of your corner office. Make a point of attending some local events for different causes and networking with your peers. Networking is a year-round goal that needs to be achieved by all corporate executives. Select some leadership conferences, luncheons, breakfasts, and trade shows and commit to attending them to shake hands, swap information, and hear industry buzz firsthand.

Seek out the "movers and shakers" within your community and introduce yourself, even if it's over the telephone. Make a point to be in touch throughout the year.

Now, if you are active within your religious community or favorite charity, this gives you another distinct group of potential contacts to help you build and maintain a network. These organizations give you personal satisfaction, the ability to enjoy your family and friends while engaging in camaraderie, and the opportunities to "give back."

Mistake #6 Self-Assessment and Improvement Plan

Jump into your community, your vendor relationships, and your industry events. Get involved in charitable events. Enormous value in personal and professional growth awaits you!

1. You know what to do here. Write down the people you need to meet and get to know.

   _____
   _____
   _____
   _____
   _____

2. Choose some community groups or causes that interest you, and write down upcoming activity dates and times.

   _____
   _____
   _____
   _____
   _____

3. Chart out an event calendar and "ink" it into your calendar. Which events or activities would you like to include?

   _____
   _____
   _____
   _____
   _____

You won't be sorry for the time and effort!

Additional Notes:

MISTAKE #7

WE CHANGE OUR ELEVATOR SPEECH.

"I can teach anybody how to get what they want out of life. The problem is that, I can't find anybody who can tell me what they want."
Mark Twain

I AM SUCH A BELIEVER IN A WELL-CRAFTED ELEVATOR SPEECH. A well-crafted elevator speech is a presentation about yourself that you enjoy giving. It should be from the heart, and be something that you are proud reciting.

I will never forget when I just so happened to be in the same networking and business meetings as a client of mine three times in one month. Yes, I heard him give his elevator speech three times that month. Each time he recited it was totally different than the time before. Each time, it was as if I didn't even know who he was and what he was looking for. Just imagine, if *I, as his Career Coach, don't understand what he is saying*, how can he expect *anyone else* to understand what he is saying? How can we expect others to help us if we don't understand, and can't articulate, what it is we want? I honestly felt like he just wasted two months of networking because two months prior, we had crafted an elevator speech that he wasn't using. But obviously, he wasn't comfortable with it, so we needed to go back to the drawing board.

So let me explain the danger of changing your elevator speech in any significant way. Remember, we talked at length in Mistake #3 about how people are not thinking about *you* in the normal course of their day. Well, they usually aren't *listening* to you, either! It's the truth! I've been observing this dynamic for a long time. Herein lies the reason that our elevator speeches need to be succinct, interesting and memorable. This is not easy to accomplish, as it takes thought, focus and creativity. But everyone can have a great elevator speech if they put their mind to it.

Here are the fundamental principles of a great elevator speech. When it's done successfully, it:

1. Gives your name and title/function.

2. Conveys you as an expert, or very knowledgeable about a certain topic. A branding statement or tagline is really useful here.

3. Shares a brief statement of accomplishment or something interesting about your experience. Seriously, this needs to be interesting!

4. Identifies what you want to do next, the industries of interest to you, and where you want to do this from a geographic perspective.

5. Invites the listener to call upon you if you can be of service or a resource to them.

6. Gives the overall impression that you are intriguing and more interesting than the other people who are giving their elevator pitches.

I am going to make the assumption that in a networking setting, you will be seeing some of the same people at more meetings to come. With this assumption, those people are going to hear you give your elevator speech more than once. I believe it takes people up to three times to finally "get" what it is someone wants to do based on their elevator speech. The first two times they hear your pitch they are not really listening, because they are still working out the components of their *own* elevator speech while you are giving yours. The *third* time, they have paid attention to enough bits and pieces that they can't help but know at least the main gist of what it is you want! So, if you keep changing your presentation...people are NEVER going to get you. If they don't GET you, they can't be helpful to you!

When you need to make your first impression count, an elevator speech that is interesting and memorable is critical. All the more reason why you need to give your elevator speech considerable thought and put in the time to make it well-rehearsed.

Oops! How to Fix Mistake #7:

Know what you want to do next and stick to your script.

Always keep your speech short and succinct, and deliver it with energy, enthusiasm and a smile. Be respectful of the fact that all of your audience is on a time schedule, watching the clock. They really are not interested in hearing a full-on monologue.

Mistake #7 Self-Assessment and Improvement Plan

1. Does your elevator speech stay on point about your professional goals? Do you state them clearly?

   _____
   _____
   _____
   _____
   _____

2. Do you feel like you need to hire a career coach or professional writer to help you create your speech?

   _____
   _____
   _____
   _____
   _____

If so, hire professionals *who are trained in job search techniques.* Anyone else may not get it right, and may have you reciting a mini life story, or focusing in on the wrong things.

Additional Notes:

MISTAKE #8

WE EXPECT HELP TO COME AT NO COST TO US.

"Operate from a position of abundance versus scarcity, and strength versus weakness."

Beth Adkisson
Vistage Chair

PEOPLE WE KNOW AND MEET don't have to extend their time and contacts to us, but they do. When I first started Power Connections, a very gracious and giving gentleman by the name of Eric Nelson took a genuine interest in my business and in helping me get it launched. Eric was in the very early stages of his own business, working on landing his first customer. His business, called Secure Privacy Solutions, was his entrepreneurial "baby." I was actually well ahead of him with a handful of clients and a small amount of revenue. By the way, anyone involved in a business where personal health information or financial data is collected, managed or shared, needs to know about the services that Eric provides.

Even knowing that I offered little to give him in return, Eric provided me with something of tremendous value—a database of names, addresses, and emails of people in my target market. This database did not come easily to him. He had individually entered all of these names from a website directory of an association to which he belongs. I am the fortunate recipient of the benefit of his membership to this association and his hours of tedious labor.

I was so touched by his generosity that I wanted to do something to show my appreciation. I knew that one of the ways I could reciprocate was to talk about his business with people I know. (Which is exactly what I am doing now.) The second way I could show him appreciation was to give him a gift, as I was certain that he wouldn't take money from me. After thinking about it for a few days, I came up with a gift that related to a conversation he and I exchanged over coffee one day.

He said he and his wife loved discovering good wines at a great value. (In other words, they enjoyed discovering cheap wine that tasted good!) It so happens that my husband and I keep a red wine in our pantry that we refer to as our "house red." It is a great red wine from Chile that we purchase for $9 a bottle. I wrapped up a bottle for Eric with a thank you card and dropped it off at his office. Later that day, he called me and I could tell that he couldn't have been more thrilled! A week later he called to report that he and his wife had tried the wine and were delighted to learn of another great tasting wine of good value!

Here are some ways that you can "pay" for the help that others give you:

Buy their coffee! Never suggest that someone meet you to discuss "your needs" and not at least offer to cover the expense of their coffee. You can afford coffee house prices—you *can't* afford to be perceived as "cheap."

The same goes for lunch. Be the first to get out the credit card and treat your resources to lunch. They don't have to spend their lunch hour with you when there are things they could be doing during that coveted time. If you meet someone after work, buy them a glass of wine and an appetizer. They could be missing dinner with their family while spending the time with you.

At the request of a well-respected business connection, I drove 90 miles to meet with a friend of his who had recently been fired from a large company. This executive picked my brain for almost two hours, asking tough questions about how to conduct an effective job search. When we were finished and the bill still lay on the table, he asked enthusiastically, "Shall we split it?" My salad was $12.00. His sandwich was $9.00.

I drove way too many miles to meet him for lunch, and to add salt to the injury, I felt that I had given away too much information. If he had simply paid for my salad, and expressed appreciation for my counsel and advice, I would have felt just fine about the drive and the giveaways. In the end, I resented him because of $12, and I was not about to extend any additional help or support during his job search.

"When someone in your network comes through, don't be a stiff. Dinner, flowers, a box of candy, a bottle of Old Faithful, a card, or even a phone call is called for. Remember, these people didn't have to extend themselves for you. But they did."

Harvey Mackay

So, be sure to express your appreciation for the help and assistance provided to you. Whenever you can, demonstrate it.

But wait! There is one more point I would like to make about operating from a position of abundance versus scarcity, and strength versus weakness:

Another way you can "pay people back" for their help when you are in transition is when you land, provide them with your contact information. It doesn't cost you a penny, but the dividends can be enormous.

What do I mean with this suggestion? If you land a job and send an announcement to people who helped you during transition, and do NOT tell them where you are now working, and your contact information, you will offend and disappoint them. By withholding your contact information you are basically saying, "When I needed you, you were there for me, but this relationship is not a two-way street. I don't want you to call or contact me now that I have a job."

Every service provider who has gone out of their way to help an executive in transition has a story about someone who took all of their help, but ignored them after they landed. This is bad business, folks. Enough said on this.

Oops! How to Fix Mistake #8:

Be generous in word and deed with fellow professionals, contacts from other companies, service providers and the outside community who helped you with your job search.

Don't even think twice about picking up the tab when they give up their valuable time to talk with you. And, what about telephone time? Yes, even telephone time deserves an acknowledgment.

Is your contact out of state? Yes, it still counts. Go online and send a token of appreciation. Or, use the good old-fashioned mail to send a hand-written thank you note and don't hesitate to enclose a gift card. I always keep a few gift cards on hand for small amounts of value, but the goodwill they generate is huge. The final caveat about thanking others for their time and help is a repeat: Don't be "cheap" about it. You don't have to spend a lot of money to show sincere gratitude.

Mistake #8 Self-Assessment and Improvement Plan

1. How do you feel about showing helpful people your appreciation?

   _____
   _____
   _____
   _____
   _____
   _____

2. In what ways do you feel most comfortable in demonstrating that?

   _____
   _____
   _____
   _____
   _____

3. Which of the following are you most likely to do in response to a valued contact's time and attention?

   _____Buy them breakfast or lunch
   _____Buy them coffee
   _____Give them a gift card
   _____Give them a bottle of wine or movie tickets
   _____Keep in touch with them once you land

MISTAKE #8

Additional Notes:

MISTAKE #9

WE FAIL TO GIVE ATTENTION AND ACKNOWLEDGMENT TO A "LESS THAN PERFECT" REPUTATION.

"What people say about you behind your back is your standing in the community."

Ed (E.W.) Howe (1853–1937)
American Journalist, Novelist

THIS DOES NOT APPLY TO most of you who read this book, but for the few of you to whom it *does* apply, I want to help you. Some of you may not be well-liked in your industry. Some of you may have disgruntled former employees who are making sure their stories are being told about your management style. Some of you may be famous for treating service providers poorly. If you read Mistake #4 and found that you have some reconciling to do with the vendor community, then it is entirely possible that you have a "less than perfect" reputation on the whole. Sorry!

These two mistakes are like bosom buddies. Whatever the case may be, you know who you are. But don't worry; your reputation is not that bad in comparison to some of the notorious business leaders we read about in the business news every day!

I could do an entire chapter about executives who berate their staff, display bad or inappropriate behavior, use poor judgment, and in general, make those who work for them miserable. But that's another book. For now, let's look at the steps you can take to repair your reputation.

Oops! How to Fix Mistake #9:

So, what can you do about this? First, admit to yourself and to a trusted advisor that you have a reputation to fix. Ask that advisor to help you, to be there for you, as you mend fences and work on changing your reputation. You will need someone to hold you accountable, brainstorm ideas, and to listen to you while you journey down this potentially rocky road.

Second, have genuine resolve to change your image. If you are not sincere about this, you will only reinforce and validate your reputation, because as soon as you land a job, you will fall back into the same negative behaviors. Considering you will be looking for another job in 2.5–3.5 years, you won't be able to repeat the charade. People will remember you as being less than honorable.

Third, get out and network as much as you can. Be helpful to as many people as you can. Word will get out that you are not such a bad person because so many people will have had a positive encounter with you!

In fact, I always say that to get to know someone is to love them. Therefore, to fix a less-than-perfect reputation, we need to become better known.

Fourth, send me an email at susan@powerconnectionsinc.com and we can set up a time to talk by telephone about your particular situation. Bad behavior and disrespect for others generates bad karma that will absolutely bite you in the "behind" when you are in need of a new job. You can change the perception that people have of you however; but it takes a strong commitment, defined strategies, and time to prove your honorable intentions. It can be done.

However, and this is a big *HOWEVER*, I caution you not to go through the motions of cleaning up your act only to do a repeat performance when you land a new job. Forgiveness and acceptance may not come again the second time around.

Mistake #9 Self-Assessment and Improvement Plan

Note to self:
_____
_____
_____
_____
_____

Additional Notes:

MISTAKE #10

WE FORGET THAT THE INTERVIEW PROCESS BEGINS IN THE PARKING LOT.

"Behavior is the mirror in which everyone shows their image."
Johann Wolfgang Von Goethe

PICTURE THIS: YOU ARRIVE EARLY FOR YOUR 2:00 P.M. INTERVIEW. You pull up to the visitor parking lot of the company where you are to be interviewed. While still in your car, you primp, comb, touch up and check to make sure your pearly whites are indeed white. You get out of your car and you tuck, button, zip and make final garment adjustments before you lock the car and begin your approach to the lobby.

Unbeknownst to you, somebody behind the reflective glass of the building is watching you—not intentionally, but by mere coincidence. It is probably someone in HR since this department is usually located near the front lobby. They take notice of you "getting yourself together" before the interview.

Or how about this: You are early for a 1:30 p.m. interview, so you decide to sit in your car in the company parking lot and make a call to your ex-wife regarding the weekend arrangements with the kids. You and she disagree on something and the conversation starts to heat up. Your voice raises and perhaps your language gets a bit strong. In the meantime, the VP of HR, whom you have never met, and who is going to be the one interviewing you at 1:30, is returning from lunch, walks by your car and hears part of your conversation. Oh, my goodness.

Another situation to consider: Your interview has gone along splendidly and as you conclude the conversation with the company executive she mentions that she has a lunch engagement offsite so she will accompany you out of the building. You are then flooded with dread that she will notice your filthy car, which is parked out front. Normally, you would drive your luxury sedan but today you are driving the family SUV. It is not only outwardly dirty but there are remnants of fast food packaging and kids' toys strewn about the backseat. You hope she doesn't get too close to your car.

The interview also starts in the lobby.

Here's another situation to consider: You arrive on time for your 3:00 p.m. interview with the president of ABC Company. The receptionist asks for your name and the reason for your visit and requests that you sign in. You oblige, but act aloof and disinterested. She asks if you would like a cup of coffee or water and you say "no."

A few minutes later, the receptionist receives a call from the president's secretary that he is going to be late. She informs you of the time delay, and you question her as to the cause for the delay, for which she has no explanation.

Sitting in the lobby, you begin to fidget and let out a few sighs. You feel frustrated that you are kept waiting. Just then the president's secretary comes out to greet you and apologizes. You break into smiles and assure her that the wait was not an inconvenience at all.

A few days later, as you are talking to someone in your network about the company, you learn that the receptionist of ABC Company is the president's daughter, who is working there part time as a summer job. You feel a pang of anxiety and wonder if she noticed your curt behavior when you were in the lobby waiting to be interviewed by her father.

These are all real-life scenarios that I have lived through with my clients or have had company representatives mention to me when we have conversed about the behaviors of candidates.

The moral of the story is this: As a candidate for a key position, it is very important that you realize that you are in someone's line of sight all the time. Realize too, that even the most inconsequential interaction with someone could prove to be significant. Everything you do and say is scrutinized. Don't think for a minute that it is not.

The job market at the executive level is challenging enough with circumstances that are beyond our control. Don't be disqualified as a candidate just because you presented a less-than-perfect attitude or you botched your interaction with an employee of the company. These are the things you CAN control. Start today with a new awareness and cognizance of your behavior, and you may find a difference in the rate of progress you are making in your job search!

Oops! How to Fix Mistake #10:

Remember that people are ALWAYS watching and listening to you. You are always "ON!"

If you absolutely must "make adjustments" as you exit your car to an interview, consider parking farther away from the building. Perhaps the few dollars invested in the parking garage is money well spent for you.

It's always good advice to arrive a few minutes early to an interview, and if it's raining or windy, you can primp lightly in the restroom with one directive: You smile and say, "Hello!" to absolutely everyone you meet as you do. The interview also starts in the restroom!

I have two more quick tips for your arrival. Remove your suit jacket and hang it up before you get behind the wheel to keep it fresh for the interview. And most important, stay off the phone! Bring a respected book to read, or use the extra time to review the notes and research you conducted about the company.

Mistake #10 Self-Assessment and Improvement Plan

1. Have you ever had moments that embarrassed you in your job search interviews? Why?

   _____
   _____
   _____
   _____
   _____

2. What is your preferred activity for passing time while waiting for a job interview to start? Does it fall into the category of "a respected read" or "reviewing company research notes?"

_____
_____
_____
_____
_____

3. If you must primp when you arrive at an interview, where do you normally do that? Have you ever thought to assess the location of your car when you are in it, leaving it, and doing one last check of yourself in the mirror?

_____
_____
_____
_____
_____

Additional Notes:

MISTAKE #11 (THE BONUS TIP)

WE DON'T BELIEVE THAT THIS ADVICE WILL WORK.

"The problem with common sense is that it is not common."
Mark Twain

LOOK, IF YOU ARE UNEMPLOYED, I WON'T LIE TO YOU. This is probably not going to be a fun time for you. Very few people enjoy their time being out of work!

You are going to have moments in your job search when you will hit the wall. You'll crash and burn. Things will come to a screeching halt and you will be convinced that this process doesn't work, or worse yet, that you'll never work again. Your significant other and family members will be looking at you with "what's up?" written all over their faces. You'll be certain you're headed for a cliff at 200 mph. *But you're not.*

There is a predictable cycle of activity in the process of job search, and it's a whole new reality for those of us who were climbing the corporate ranks in recent years. The job search world we knew then has left the building.

We flew high and fast, earning promotions, progressive salaries, and fat bonuses—without ever needing to toil over a résumé or elevator pitch. We were having fabulous offsite meetings and corporate retreats at top hotels, and company parties at five-star restaurants.

Life was all about up, up, up…until you walked into your office one Friday morning and you couldn't log on to your computer. Or the security guard was standing at your office door. Or you were greeted by a human resources representative for an unscheduled meeting. Or your boss calls you out of the blue and requests that you come into his/her office with no explanation as to what they want to talk to you about. Rarely ever did we experience the rumor of a forthcoming round of pink slips, and everyone ducking their heads and glancing over their shoulders, wondering what was about to happen.

And here you are. For many of you, this is the first time you'll be on the outside of the executive suite looking in. It is simply awful when it happens to you.

The "Good" News about the Process.

Just about every executive has been laid off or fired at some point in their career. Believe it or not, you just joined an elite club! Like those before you, you will pick yourself up, dust yourself off, and find another job.

Your job search will test your mettle. It will test everything you know about yourself, your confidence, and your esteem. It will test your relationships. It will humble you and perhaps give you a new resolve about the meaning of your life purpose and how you want to move into the future.

But, as they say, "It's always the darkest before the dawn." There's no question you will find work. It's just a question of *when*.

Oops! How to Fix Mistake #11:

Trust the process. The light at the end of the tunnel will come! It is just a matter of time.

Hire a career transition coach to see you through, step by step. Spend time with the professionals who can help you: a professional résumé writer, an interview coach, a speech coach if you need one, and an image consultant. The resources abound. Get physical and dental checkups to be at your best.

If you are a person of faith, be active in your religious organization or get involved with charity and community groups. Resurrect or find a sense of purpose.

Sharpen your professional saw. Keep up with your professional and academic credentials and industry buzz.

Mistake #11 Self-Assessment and Improvement Plan

1. Do you need to remind yourself that life is not just about you? Can you see how helping others will increase your connections, bolster your self esteem, and give you new avenues of finding possible

opportunities? What are some ways you can reach out and help others?

_____
_____
_____
_____
_____

2. Get out of your own way and commit to the process. How can you use this transitional period of your life to learn things about yourself; reconnect with your family, friends, community and passions; and emerge as a stronger and more focused executive?

_____
_____
_____
_____
_____

3. Identify the resources you can deploy to give yourself a competitive edge in the job market.

_____
_____
_____
_____
_____

MISTAKE #11 (THE BONUS TIP)

Additional Notes:

Conclusion

For most of us, job search is hard work because there are so many business conditions and behind-the-scenes situations that affect the job search process. These elements can perceivably render us powerless to affect the outcome of our efforts. The message I would like to impart to you is more than making you aware of specific pitfalls of certain behaviors people have demonstrated in job search. It's an overarching message that everything you do in your business life now, and everything you have done in your business life in the past, matters. The good, the bad, and the ugly are all exacerbated when you are looking for a job.

Your business reputation, and the manner in which you are conducting yourself during job search, take on a life of their own. Their confluence becomes another dynamic of job search that you will have to manage.

There is an expression about life that is worth stating in this book: "Wherever you go, there you are."

Job search is not so much a "destination" as a process that's started while you are still employed. The image you project to the professional community starts while you're working.

Let your image be one that causes you no recovery time during job search. Cultivate a reputation and an image that is a springboard to creating healthy and helpful relationships that will be a part of your networking and business community for years to come.

I have noticed through the years in my work with executives in transition that there are certain clients who seem to go through the job search process with less tension and stress. This particular group always seemed to have a pipeline of activities and appeared to actually enjoy themselves. Yes, they had their moments of disappointment and frustration, but there was something different about these people.

One day I decided to write down what it was about these certain clients that made them stand out from the rest. Here is what I came up with:

10 Characteristics of Executives Who Have the Most Successful Job Search Experiences:

1. They developed professional relationships throughout their career.

2. They possess a good reputation; people think positively of them.

3. They have great references and a variety of people to endorse them.

4. They have a history of repeated success.

5. They have an easily defined skill set.

6. They have healthy *personal* relationships. They love others.

7. They have an open and reflective perspective.

8. They have a positive attitude and they are quick to "move on" after disappointment.

9. They have a lot of confidence, but rarely, if ever, show arrogance.

10. They have an appreciative and thoughtful approach.

A job search is tough enough without sabotaging our own steps. Let's give ourselves the benefit of doing as many things *right* as we possibly can. So, control what you can, and manage as graciously as you can the things you can't control.

I guarantee you the world will respond in kind.

About the Author

Susan Howington is a sought-after expert in the Executive Career Transition field, applying her practical knowledge and visionary wisdom as a coach and industry speaker. She is the Founder and CEO of Power Connections, a national Executive Outplacement, Coaching and Leadership Development Company. Her background as a corporate executive and entrepreneur serving Fortune 100 companies gives her personal knowledge of what drives and challenges business leaders. Susan's business success in helping executives derives from her understanding that in circumstances of executive job search, nothing replaces an individualized and customized search strategy, and the effectiveness of human interaction and person-to-person connections.

After graduating with a B.S. in Sociology and a minor in Psychology from Northern Arizona University in Flagstaff, Arizona, Susan landed her first professional job as a drug and alcohol counselor with the Mohave Mental Health Clinic. Throughout her life, she has had a deep interest in human behavior, accompanied by an industrious drive to pursue working in commercial business enterprises.

Susan's work has captured the attention of the Orange County, California, *OC Metro Magazine* as one of its *15 Orange County Women Who Inspire Others*. News media around the country have featured Susan in their stories about executive job transition. She has appeared in newspapers such as *The Orange County Register* and *Los Angeles Times*, national online publications like *ABC7 New York*, *CBS2 Chicago*, and *Fox Business News*, as well as *CareerBuilder.com*, to name a few.

Susan can be reached at susan@powerconnectionsinc.com. Her website is www.PowerConnectionsInc.com.

Services provided by Susan Howington and the Power Connections team of experts include:

Executive Coaching & Leadership Development

Executive Outplacement

Expatriate Support

Selection Support

Executive Team Building

Presentations provided by Susan Howington include:

- How Smart People Sabotage their Job Search: 10 Mistakes Executives Make and How to Fix Them!

- You've Still Got It! Job Search Tips for the Over-50 Executive

- Life and Job Search Success: What's Love, Luck and Karma Got to Do With It?

- How to Turn Networking into Meaningful Connections

- Strategic HR Leader: Are You One?

Visit our website at www.PowerConnectionsInc.com

Suggested Reading and Reference Sources

Kerr, Cherie. *How to BE Presidential: The Secret Handbook for Top-Level Executives and Those Who Aspire to Be.* Santa Ana, CA: Execuprov Press, 2010.

Ferrazzi, Keith. *Never Eat Alone.* New York: Random House, 2005.

Mackay, Harvey. *Dig Your Well Before You're Thirsty: The Only Networking Book You'll Ever Need.* New York: Currency Doubleday, 1997.

Meshel, Jeff. *One Phone Call Away: Secrets of a Master Networker.* New York: The Penguin Group, 2005.

Share your experiences with us!

Have you experienced some unique, embarrassing or surprising job search situations that you'd like to share with us? Would you like to tell us about an "Oops!" you made in your job search? We'd love to hear about it!

What about the mistakes you've seen *someone else* make in their job search? If you have observed some foibles that you think are noteworthy, or could make history as being classified as one of the biggest mistakes ever, we'd be interested in hearing those, too. Just remember to change the names to protect the guilty!

Send your stories to susan@powerconnectionsinc.com.

Additional Notes:

Additional Notes:

Additional Notes:

Additional Notes:

Made in the USA
San Bernardino, CA
28 December 2015